The Challenge of
MINERAL
RESOURCES

ROBERT L. BATES

.

✦ *Environmental Issues Series* ✦

E N S L O W   P U B L I S H E R S ,   I N C .

Bloy St. & Ramsey Ave.
Box 777
Hillside, N.J. 07205
U.S.A.

P.O. Box 38
Aldershot
Hants GU12 6BP
U.K.

This book is dedicated to all who are interested in the wise use of the resources of our bountiful planet Earth.

Library of Congress Cataloging-in-Publication Data

Bates, Robert Latimer, 1912-

The challenge of mineral resources / Robert L. Bates.

p. cm. —(Environmental issues series)

Includes bibliographical references and index.

Summary: Explores mineral resources and mining in terms of science, technology, society, and environmental impact.

ISBN 0-89490-245-8

1. Mines and mineral resources—Juvenile literature. 2. Mineral industries—Environmental aspects—Juvenile literature. [1. Mines and mineral resources.] I. Title. II. Series: Environmental issues series (Hillside, N.J.)

TN148.B36 1991
553—dc20   90-35948
                                              CIP
                                              AC

Printed in the United States of America

10 9 8 7 6 5 4 3 2 1

Illustration Credits:
Robert L. Bates, pp. 8, 9, 11, 13, 16, 23, 26, 31, 38, 50; Dresser Industries, Inc., p. 30; Ohio Geological Survey, pp. 10, 22, 28, 34; Royal Botanical Gardens, Hamilton, Ont., p. 40; Secured Data Services Inc., p. 54; Society for Mining, Metallurgy, and Exploration, Inc., p. 19; U.S. Bureau of Mines, p. 43; Jerry D. Vineyard, p. 54.

Cover Photo:
Ohio Geological Survey

Contents

1

Introduction

On a wooded ridge in eastern Ohio, the ground is pitted with shallow trenches. Here the Wyandots and other Native American tribes dug flint for their arrowheads, spears, and scrapers. The flint, a hard dense rock that breaks with sharp edges, was traded widely among the tribes of eastern North America. To these primitive people, flint was an important mineral resource.

Today we don't need flint for arrowheads, but we do need crushed stone for concrete, iron ore for steel, crude oil for gasoline, and many other earth-derived materials. In fact, we are far more dependent on the earth's mineral resources than the Native Americans ever were. We mine rocks and minerals by the millions of tons. We produce crude oil by the millions of barrels. We put these raw materials through elaborate refining processes to obtain the products we want. Without mineral resources, our complex industrialized society could not operate.

Society is faced with three major challenges. The first challenge is to find the necessary deposits of oil, ore, or other raw material—and to keep on finding new deposits as the old ones are used up. These tasks are the province of geologists, geophysicists, and other earth scientists.

5

The second challenge is technological: to get the raw material out of the ground and process it into a useful form. Mining and petroleum engineers concentrate on production; metallurgical and chemical engineers, on processing.

The third challenge is to protect the environment and conserve mineral resources. This is a job for everyone.

This book is designed to show how science, technology, and society interact to affect mineral-resource issues. This way of looking at the issues will give you a broad base of understanding about our mineral resources and help you think about solutions to some of the problems connected with them.

2

The Nature of Mineral Resources

Rocks, ores, and oil pools are our three major mineral resources. Rock is generally defined as an aggregate, or mass, of different minerals. Ore is a body of rock from which one or more valuable minerals may be extracted at a profit. Oil pools are porous rocks that contain crude oil. Each is a source of valuable earth materials.

Rocks

What solid material from the earth's crust has the largest number of essential uses? The answer has to be limestone, a common sedimentary rock. Formed of sea shells and shell fragments in solidified limy mud, limestone has both physical and chemical uses. At a few places it is cut and carved for building stone. Countrywide, millions of tons are crushed for use in concrete, and millions more go into the making of cement. Limestone is the source of lime (calcium oxide, CaO). This simple compound is one of the four mainstays of the vast chemical industry (the others being salt, sulfur, and coal or petroleum). Lime is also used in steelmaking, sugar refining, soil improvement, and paper

7

manufacture. Strange as it may seem, modern industrial life would be impossible without limestone.

Other sedimentary rocks are important, too. Sand and sandstone yield silica for glass. Shale and clay make building bricks and drainage tiles. Special types of clay go into table china, high-quality glossy paper, oil-well drilling fluid, and foundry molds for casting metal. Two sedimentary rocks, one rich in phosphorus and the other in potassium, provide fertilizer for the world's croplands. Coal generates electricity for our homes and factories and is also a chemical raw material.

Two igneous rocks are useful resources. Basalt is a dark, slaggy lava, formed in times past by volcanic eruptions. It is quarried and crushed for use in concrete and highways. Granite is a coarse-grained rock that cooled slowly underground and is exposed where overlying rocks have been eroded away. It is cut and trimmed for panels, columns, and steps and is much used in monuments and memorials. The Vietnam Memorial in Washington, D.C., is made of dark granite from India.

A high-purity limestone, made up mostly of fossil shells.

8

Among the metamorphic rocks, marble and slate are of modest importance. Marble was formed by the squeezing and recrystallization of limestone at depth in the earth's crust. Most marble is white, often with streaks of gray. It is easily cut and carved, and it takes a fine polish. Marble is used, as it has been for centuries, on public buildings and in statues and memorials. Slate was produced by the tight folding and shearing of deeply buried shale beds. A compact, dense rock, slate can be split into thin sheets well suited for roofing and for rectangular floor tiles.

Ore Deposits

An ore deposit is a body of rock from which one or more valuable minerals, generally metallic, can be extracted at a profit. In this definition, note the phrase "at a profit." Finding and mining ore deposits are difficult and expensive. No one undertakes the job just for amusement; it must be a money-making operation. This means that an ore deposit is not only a geologic feature but an economic one as well. Its value is tied to the price of the metal derived from it. A body of rock that is an ore deposit today may be waste rock tomorrow if the

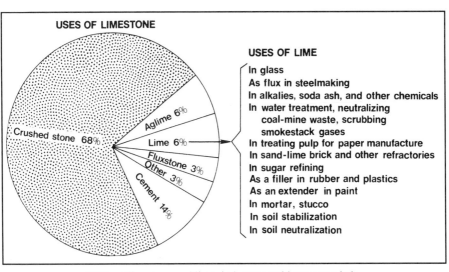

Without limestone and lime, industry would come to a halt.

price of the metal goes down so that mining is no longer profitable. Conversely, today's body of worthless rock may be tomorrow's ore deposit if the price of the metal goes up. That is what happened with gold in the 1970s.

Ore deposits have formed in many different ways. The world's great deposits of iron ore are of sedimentary origin. Bauxite, the ore of aluminum, formed by long-continued weathering of granitic rocks in a humid climate. Rich deposits of nickel and chromium ore, and low-grade deposits of copper ore, are found in bodies of igneous rock where they originated.

When hot waters of igneous origin move through rocks, they may leave metal-bearing minerals behind as they cool. The solutions may deposit their minerals in open fractures, forming veins or vein systems.

A limestone quarry. Dust comes from the machine, which is drilling a shot hole for blasting. The thickness of the overburden in the background suggests that quarrying may soon give way to mining beneath the hill.

10

California's famous Mother Lode is a complex system of gold-quartz veins. Or such waters may dissolve limestone, at the same time replacing it with ore minerals. Rich deposits of lead and zinc minerals in Missouri have been formed by this replacement process. Ore-bearing solutions soaking through rocks with very small pore spaces may leave tiny, scattered grains of an introduced mineral. The "invisible gold" of Nevada was formed in this way.

Most of the metallic elements occur in nature combined with other elements. Iron, for example, is found in the mineral hematite (iron oxide), copper in chalcocite (copper sulfide), and so on. But there is one metallic element—one glorious element—that is a mineral all by

"Coontail ore" in a mine in southern Illinois. Light bands are fluorspar (calcium fluoride, CaF_2), a source of fluorine for chemicals and ceramics. Dark bands contain metallic sulfides and other minerals. The beds above and below are limestone.

itself. That element/mineral is gold. Not only does gold occur alone, but it is also chemically stable, remaining unchanged even though the rocks in which it occurs are uplifted, weathered, and eroded. Gold freed by weathering may be washed into streams, where it mixes with the ordinary sand and gravel along the stream channel. Gold is in tiny grains or small flakes, only rarely in nuggets the size of a raisin or larger. Stream gravels that contain workable deposits of gold or other valuable minerals are called placer deposits, or simply placers. (This word is from the Spanish and rhymes with passer.) Other minerals found in placer deposits are the oxides of tin and titanium.

Oil Pools

The first thing to note about oil pools is that they are not pools in the everyday sense. An oil pool is a body of porous and permeable rock that contains crude oil. This oil holds natural gas in solution; in some pools a separate accumulation of gas is present above the oil, and a few pools contain gas alone. We will use the term oil pool to refer to all these occurrences.

Oil is found in regions underlain by thick accumulations of sedimentary rocks. These rocks almost always have a very slight inclination, or regional dip. They may have been affected by slight to moderate folding and faulting, but not by intense deformation as in mountain belts. Very little oil is found in mountainous regions.

The rock that contains an oil pool is termed the reservoir rock. The most common reservoir rocks are sandstone, with open spaces between the sand grains, and limestone, with fractures or solution passages.

How does crude oil form? Its parent material was probably the remains of microscopic floating plants and animals, called plankton, that lived and died in ancient seas. A steady rain of dead plankton fell onto the seafloor. Preserved in a stagnant mud without oxygen, it was transformed into crude oil. This change was probably produced by bacteria, aided by heat from the earth, but scientists are not sure about that. As the muds were buried by younger sediments and compacted into shale, the oil was squeezed out into more porous rocks.

Except for a zone just below the ground surface, rocks in most regions are saturated with water to a great depth. Since oil is lighter than water, any oil generated in the deep parts of sedimentary basins tends to move upward. It moves toward the top of any porous layer that it enters, and within that layer it moves up the regional dip. The movement of oil, in short, is antigravity.

A pool forms when the upward movement of oil is stopped by some obstruction, and the oil backs up as though behind a dam. It displaces some or most of the water in the pore spaces. Any feature in the rocks that impedes the upward movement of oil and causes it to

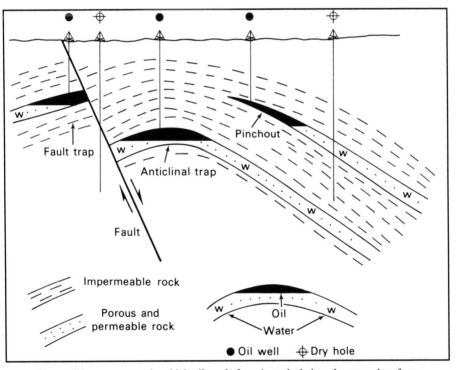

Three of the many ways in which oil pools form in rocks below the ground surface. Oil in a reservoir rock (dotted) accumulates below an impermeable roof rock (dashed).

form a pool is a trap. There are many kinds of traps. Among these are coral reefs, now dead and buried; ancient shorelines and deltas, their porous sands covered by impervious shale; sandstone beds that gradually thin and disappear, or "pinch out" as oilmen say, toward the margin of the basin; and sandstones that grade laterally into shale. More spectacular are traps made by earth forces acting on the rocks long after they were deposited. The best known, and earliest recognized, of all traps is the anticline. This is a gentle upward fold or dome; typically, shale acts as a "roof rock," trapping oil in a porous reservoir rock below. Other traps are formed by various types of faults.

Then there are the remarkable features called salt domes. In the Gulf Coast region of Louisiana and Texas, some 30,000 feet (9,100 meters) of sand, silt, and clay beds have been penetrated from below by pillars or columns of salt. The salt has risen by solid flow, like the ice of a glacier. It has come from a thick "mother salt" bed at great depth. The salt is unstable, as it is lighter than the sediments above it. Hundreds of traps—pinch-outs, anticlines, and faults, among others—have been formed in the sandstone/shale sequence of sediments by the intrusion of more than 200 salt domes. Owing to great quantities of oil and innumerable traps, the Gulf Coast is one of the world's most productive oil regions.

The term *oil field* refers to an area underlain by an oil pool or by two or more related pools, along with the pumps, tanks, and related production equipment. Some fields include only half a dozen wells or so, on a few acres; at the other extreme are fields like East Texas, which has thousands of wells on 200 square miles (520 square kilometers) of land. Depth to the oil ranges widely. One of America's richest oil fields, the Yates field of western Texas, produces oil from only 1,000 to 1,100 feet (300 to 350 meters). This depth is practically at the grass roots, as they say in the oil business. Wells in California and the Gulf Coast may be twenty times as deep. The thickness of the reservoir rock may be a few feet to a few hundred feet. Porosity ranges from slight to cavernous.

3

How Do We Find Mineral Resources?

Since mineral resources are parts of the earth's crust and this crust is highly complex, geologists are called on to locate usable deposits. Let's look at the methods that these earth scientists use in finding valuable rocks, ore deposits, and oil pools.

Hunting for a Rock

Here is an assignment that was handed to a firm of consulting geologists in 1962. A big cement company decided to construct a new plant in the east-central United States. Where should they locate it? The company's management laid down these requirements:

1. The site must be within 100 miles (160 kilometers) of St. Louis, Missouri.
2. The plant must be no more than 3,000 feet (900 meters) from a navigable river.
3. Major rail lines and highways should pass through the site.
4. The raw-material deposit must contain 250 million tons of limestone and about 60 million tons of clay or shale.

5. The limestone must contain at least 90 percent calcium carbonate ($CaCO_3$), and no more than 3.5 percent magnesium oxide (MgO), 2.5 percent iron oxide (Fe_2O_3), and 5.0 percent silica (SiO_2). The shale or clay must be low in MgO, high in alumina (Al_2O_3), moderately high in Fe_2O_3, and must contain silica in the 45 to 60 percent range.

In order to meet the first requirement, the deposit would have to

Sandstone suitable for making glass. The rock is more than 96 percent quartz (silica, SiO_2). Finding high-purity deposits like this one is a job for the geologist.

be either in Missouri or across the Mississippi River in Illinois. Therefore, the first step was to consult the geological surveys of those two states. Twenty-nine possible sites were selected. They were examined by plane, by car, by boat, and by sampling the stone in active quarries. By these means, twenty-one of the twenty-nine sites were ruled out. Of the eight remaining, five were eliminated after cores showed that the raw material was not of the required quality. The three remaining sites were extensively core-drilled. At one, there was too much MgO; at another, the stone contained pockets of chert, or flint, an undesirable silica rock. One promising locality was left, at Clarksville, Missouri, 70 miles (112 kilometers) north of St. Louis

A detailed map of this site was made by air surveying. Forty-six deep core holes were drilled. A geophysical study gave a detailed subsurface map of the limestone and the overlying shale. As a result of all these efforts, it was decided to accept the site for the quarry and plant. Production of cement started in January 1968.

A lot of money, a lot of work, and a long lead time—nearly six years—were needed between the company's decision to locate a plant and shipment of the first ton of finished cement. Limestone is a common rock, but large-scale development for cement raw material or any other product is not just a matter of finding a convenient ledge and starting a quarry. Knowing where to look for required rock deposits and how to evaluate them is a job for the exploration geologist.

Finding Ore Deposits

On January 24, 1848, workmen were enlarging John Sutter's lumber mill on the south fork of the American River 40 miles (65 kilometers) east of Sacramento, California. They decided that the stream channel needed deepening in order to bring more water to the mill wheel. In channeling the sand, they saw bright flakes and specks of gold. They then forgot about lumber and started to work the placer deposit for the yellow metal.

Placer mining in or beside a rushing stream is hard work. Shoveling some sand into a broad pan, a man would submerge the pan in the stream and swirl it slowly, washing the light sand and silt out over the rim. After a few minutes, the pan would be clear of everything but a spoonful of residue—heavy minerals. With a skillful motion, the prospector would spread out this material on the bottom of the pan. If he was in luck, there would be a little tail of gold specks at the end. (Gold is nineteen times as heavy as water and far heavier than any of the common minerals, so it would be the very last material to be washed or moved in the pan.) The grains of gold would be picked out with a knife or fingernail. After a hard day's work, a man could make a bare living wage from a lean placer, or several hundred dollars from a rich one.

The word from Sutter's mill spread fast. Within two years, more than 40,000 men had joined the gold rush to California. These "forty-niners," as they came to be called, prospected every stream channel along the west front of the Sierra Nevada range. Eventually they traced the placer gold upstream to its bedrock source. This, the Mother Lode, proved to be a belt of gold-quartz veins extending for 70 miles (112 kilometers) along the western foothills of the Sierra Nevada.

Every likely-looking stream in the great west, from the Rocky Mountains to the Pacific Coast, was soon tested. In 1859, George Jackson made a lucky strike in Clear Creek, Colorado: a placer deposit that would yield $100 million in the next sixty years. (Like most prospectors, Jackson didn't stay around to develop the deposit, but sold out for a modest sum, probably a few thousand dollars.) The Clear Creek find and an even richer one at Cripple Creek were exaggerated in the eastern newspapers and started another westward stampede of gold seekers. By 1879, Colorado has surpassed California as a producer of gold.

In 1859, placer miners at Gold Hill, a desolate part of the Washoe Mountains of Nevada, were running short of water for their gold pans.

They dug a small reservoir. At about 4 feet (1.2 meters) they dug into a soft, dark sandy rock, which when washed was found to be rich in pale yellow gold dust. A sample was sent to California for testing, or assaying. At first, the assayer could not believe his results: the stuff tested at $3,000 in silver and $876 in gold per ton! The result of this strike was one of the world's richest and most famous mining districts, the Comstock Lode. It yielded over $400 million during the next three decades, from more than 100 mines.

A similar story could be told about many western ore deposits. First came discovery of gold in placer gravels—"the poor man's

The old-time prospector, as seen by a modern artist.

mine." Then the bedrock source was found, and one or more underground lode mines were developed. Most of these mines had a life of only a few years, or at most a few decades, as shown by numerous ghost towns scattered through the mountains from Colorado to California. An exception is the Homestake mine, in the Black Hills of South Dakota. Started in 1870, it is still one of North America's major producers of gold. In 1875, a rich deposit of copper ore was found at Butte, Montana, by miners working a silver deposit. Butte shortly became the world's largest single producer of copper and remained an important source of that metal for more than 100 years.

In early 1961, a large deposit of gold ore was discovered in north-central Nevada. This was a surprising event because that area of mountains and desert had been combed by prospectors for decades. But the gold is in a dark, impure limestone, which would hardly have rated a glance by a prospector. Furthermore, the ore mineral is in grains less than 0.0004 inch (0.01 millimeter) in diameter. This invisible gold is dispersed, or disseminated, through large bodies of limestone. The total amount present makes this a world-class deposit, or rather a series of several related deposits. It is known as the Carlin Trend.

The Carlin discovery was a joint geological effort. In the late 1950s, Ralph Roberts, a geologist with the United States Geological Survey, had studied the complex geology of this part of Nevada. In a report published in 1960, he suggested that certain areas might be promising targets for exploration. Large-scale mapping and sampling of one of these areas were begun in the spring of 1961, under the direction of John Livermore, a company geologist. Exploratory drilling began in July 1962, and the first ore-grade material was found in September. In the next two and a half years, 11 million tons of ore, with about 0.3 ounce (8.5 grams) of gold per ton, was confirmed in this one deposit. A mine went into production in 1965.

Three-tenths of an ounce of gold per ton of rock doesn't seem like much, but at the government-established price of $35 per ounce, this deposit had a value of well over $100 million. Then in March 1968, for the first time gold was allowed to be traded in the open market. By 1975, the price had gone up to $161 per ounce, and in 1980 it was over $600! In the middle and late 1980s, the price was in the $350 to $400 range—more than ten times what it was when mining started. Not surprisingly, several other deposits are now being mined. The ore deposits of the Carlin Trend, plus market forces, have given new meaning to the old Spanish term *bonanza*: a rich deposit of ore.

The Search for Oil

You can collect a rock specimen from an ore deposit, but not from an oil pool. Oil pools are hidden. Oil underground can be reached only by the drill.

The search for oil began in the mid-1800s. It was guided in part by chance. For example, oil might appear in a well drilled for water—to the disgust of the farmer, who needed the water for his cattle. More commonly, prospectors drilled where oil seeped from the ground. Oil seeps were common along creek banks, and for a while the search for likely places to drill was known as "creekology."

It was soon noticed that oil seeps and oil pools were often present along the crests of anticlines. By 1875, the "anticlinal theory" of oil accumulation was firmly established. Other types of traps remained unsought and unknown for some twenty-five years.

We should remember that until about 1900 the main product needed from crude oil was kerosene, for the nation's lamps. But by 1901, there were 14,800 automobiles registered in the United States. In the new century, a skyrocketing demand for gasoline and motor oil was assured.

Oil was found at first by a combination of practical experience and sheer superstition. Besides looking for seeps and anticlines, wildcatters—as prospectors for oil came to be called—relied on the divining rod. Termed a wiggle stick by oil men, this was usually a forked branch that supposedly would twist downward when held over underground water or oil. Ingenious persons invented various electric or chemical gadgets, known as doodlebugs.

By 1920, however, large oil companies had been organized, and most of them had exploration departments. Geologists were learning

A gusher. The wooden derrick tells us that this event happened a long time ago. The picture was taken in the 1890s.

how to locate other traps besides the obvious anticlines. Several valuable tools for this search had been developed.

A prime source of information was the drilled well. Samples of the rock penetrated in every well were systematically taken, generally at 10-foot (3-meter) depth intervals. These samples, or rock cuttings, were described and the results plotted on a sample log, a strip of paper representing the well.

The sample log was soon joined by other types. One is the electric log. After a hole is drilled, a record of the rocks penetrated is made by measuring the electric current flowing between an electrode moving up the well and a grounded electrode at the surface. Each rock layer tends to give a characteristic curve. Another method records the rocks' radioactivity. Most limestones, for example, are weakly radioactive;

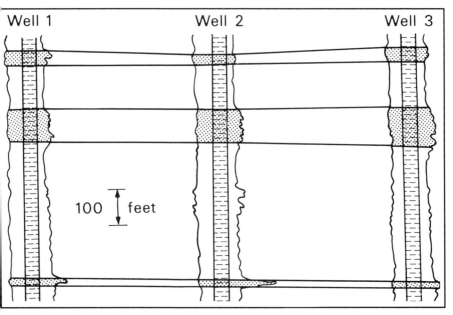

Strata encountered in wells drilled for oil may be readily identified from well to well. The central column for each well is the sample log, showing by standard patterns the rocks penetrated. The wiggly lines are electric logs. Although these wells may be miles apart, this combination of well records makes matching up precise and accurate.

many shales, in contrast, give a pronounced reaction. Even the rocks' reaction to sound waves may be recorded in a sonic log.

Another technique that enables the geologist to see into the subsurface is seismic surveying. A series of geophones, which are very sensitive sound pickups, are spaced out along a line on the ground. They are connected to a truck-mounted recording device. An explosion then produces a man-made mini-earthquake. The shock wave travels downward into the crust. Each resistant rock layer reflects some of the wave energy back to the surface. The geophones pick up each of these reflected waves. The resulting seismogram shows the attitude and thickness of the rocks down to a depth of several thousand feet. The procedure is repeated to make a cross-country traverse that may be many miles long.

The long-term object of such studies is to put together as complete a regional picture as possible to guide future prospecting. The short-term object is to locate a subsurface feature that looks as though it might be a trap for oil. If such an anomaly is found, an exploratory well, termed a wildcat, will tell whether the geologist's interpretation was correct.

Even with all modern prospecting techniques, at least four out of five wildcats are dry holes—they find either no oil or not enough to be of commercial interest. But a dry hole is not a total loss. The log will add to the store of geological information. If the well yields a little oil or gas, this may be an indication that the well is close to a pool.

If the wildcat well makes a discovery, the geologist has new problems to consider. What kind of trap is it? Where is this well located on the trap? Which way should we move to drill the next well? Finding the answers to such questions as these is the challenge in developing a new source of oil.

4

Producing Mineral Wealth

Every year in this country, about one billion tons of rock are quarried and crushed. Much of this enormous tonnage goes into road bases and ready-mix paving, and especially into concrete. By far the most widely used rock is limestone, along with its cousin dolomite. Where these are unavailable, granite or basalt may be used. And here we must switch from the geological word *rock* to the commercial term *stone*. Stone is any rock that is put to physical use.

At a typical quarry, soil and unusable material are removed by scrapers and trucks. Then shallow holes are drilled a few feet back from the quarry face, and explosives are placed in them. A blast brings down several thousand tons onto the quarry floor. Trucks take the broken stone across the quarry to a crusher, which breaks it into pieces no longer than 8 inches (20.3 centimeters) across.

From here the stone is moved by conveyor belt up to the plant on the surface level. This consists of a maze of crushing, washing, and screening equipment. From this plant emerge a dozen or more grades of stone, from the size of your fist down to that of coarse sand. The stone is loaded out by truck to the road-building job or other point of use. Stone also goes by belt to a ready-mix concrete plant next door, and the finer grades to a plant that produces blacktop for streets and roads.

A competitor of crushed stone is sand and gravel. Since nature has done the crushing, this loose material needs no blasting and can be readily screened into size grades.

Limestone is the main raw material of cement. Finely crushed, the stone is introduced into a ball mill. This is a big steel drum partly filled with steel balls about the size of a billiard ball. As the drum rotates, the balls grind the stone to a fine powder. The limestone is combined with similarly ground clay or shale, and the mix is partly melted in intense heat. The resulting "clinker," when cooled and finely ground, is cement.

When pure crushed limestone is heated in a kiln at about 1,093° C (2,000° F), its constituent calcite is decomposed. Forty-four percent disappears as carbon dioxide gas, CO_2; and 56 percent remains as white

Underground space of possible future value. It is in a still-active limestone mine.

porous lumps of lime, CaO. This, as we saw earlier, is one of the most widely used compounds in industry. A similar heating procedure, when applied to dolomite, yields lime-magnesia, CaO • MgO. This substance goes into bricks that are highly resistant to heat.

Certain high-purity limestones, and also some white marbles, are ground extremely fine for use in paint, plastics, putty, and other products.

Massive bodies of uniform and attractive stone, found in a few localities, can be quarried in large blocks and cut into a variety of shapes for use in building. The most common of these dimension stones are limestone, sandstone, granite, marble, and slate. Procedures differ with each type of stone, and indeed with each deposit. In general, big blocks are separated from the parent ledge, are lifted from the quarry by a derrick, and are moved to the nearby mill by truck or rail. Here they are cut into desired thicknesses, by saws of various types. Carving, lettering, and other decoration is done by skilled craftsmen. Dimension stone is produced to order, for specific building or construction projects.

A horizontal rock layer may be quarried into the side of a hill until the overburden becomes too thick to handle. A tunnel may then be opened and a mine developed under the hill. Stone underground is commonly mined by the room-and-pillar method. About half the rock is removed, leaving big rooms, and the rest is left as pillars to support the roof. Only a small proportion of ordinary crushed stone comes from underground mines, but such mines provide most of our salt and potassium-rich rocks. Some potassium-bearing strata are mined by machines that bore big passages through the rock.

Soluble rocks such as salt are also obtained by solution mining, which requires no underground work but is done from the surface. Wells are drilled into the salt beds, and water is pumped down to dissolve the salt before returning to the surface. The brine that results may be evaporated to yield solid salt, or introduced directly into processes of chemical manufacture.

Coal is a unique rock and poses unique problems. Near-surface beds are uncovered by stripping the overburden, which in some districts is many feet thick. Stripping is done by big machines that can scoop up 50 cubic yards (38 cubic meters) or more of soil and rock at one pass, swing around, and deposit the material in a worked-out part of the mine. Then power shovels are moved in to dig out the coal. Strip mining has long been a despoiler of land, water, and vegetation, but today operators are required to restore mined land to productive use.

Coal beds underground are mined most commonly by the longwall method. Temporary support at a long working face is supplied by steel columns. The roof caves in as mining progresses and the columns are moved forward. The process is highly automated. Almost all the coal

A coal bed 42 inches (100 centimeters) thick, ready for removal in a strip mine. More than 100 feet (30 meters) of overlying rocks may be removed in order to reach a bed of this thickness.

is removed, in contrast with the room-and-pillar method. The mining company may be required to pay property owners for damages if their land subsides over a coal mine.

However obtained, coal must be transported to its point of use, commonly a power-generating plant. The most frequently used means of transport is the unit train—as many as a hundred hopper cars that are never separated but shuttle back and forth between mine and power plant. The cars are loaded and unloaded automatically.

From Mine to Metal

Twenty miles southwest of Salt Lake City, Utah, at a place called Bingham Canyon, there is an immense hole in the ground. Shaped like an inverted cone, it is half a mile (0.8 kilometer) deep and 2 miles (3.2 kilometers) across. This feature is a copper mine.

The open pit at Bingham Canyon is in an ordinary-looking rock called porphyry. This fine-grained igneous rock contains a few percent of copper-bearing sulfide minerals in very small grains scattered through the rock. It is a low-grade ore, which must be mined on a large scale in order to be profitable.

Bingham Canyon is one of several porphyry copper deposits along the western mountain belts of North and South America. Typically, at such deposits, the rock is blasted down on 50-foot (15-meter) benches, which give the pit a terraced appearance. After preliminary crushing, trainloads of ore go to the mill. Procedures at these big open-pit mines are much like those at a stone quarry: strip, drill, blast, crush, load out to the mill. Open-pit mining is really a large-scale earthmoving operation.

Underground mining is a more complicated matter. At the Comstock Lode (Chapter 3), the ore bodies were found to be separated by unstable, treacherous rock. A method of mining was developed that used wooden supports, in a framework known as square-set timbering. In Missouri's Viburnum Trend, by contrast, lead and zinc ore occurs in massive strong limestone, and mining is by the room-and-pillar method. Ore veins are generally mined in openings called stopes. The specific method used depends on the nature of the ore, the steepness and dimensions of the vein, the type of enclosing rock, and related factors.

In the mineral industries, a mill is where things are taken apart: it is a disassembly line. The first step is to grind up the ore. A common method of separating ore minerals from waste rock is flotation. The mill feed, as the ground-up ore is called, is stirred up in water, and a chemical reagent is added. This attaches itself to the grains of metallic sulfides, but ignores the grains of quartz and other nonmetallic minerals. It gives the sulfide grains a coating that repels water. In the

A continuous-mining machine. The toothed drum at the top rotates as it moves down the mine face. Ore is dislodged, falls on pan below, and is gathered by rotating arms onto the conveyor belt. This carries it to a truck or tram at the rear. The machine weighs about 100 tons and is best adapted to relatively soft rocks such as salt, borax, or potash.

next stage a frothing agent, such as pine oil or soap, is added. As the feed is stirred up, the sulfide grains stick to the bubbles, rising with them to form a froth at the top of the flotation cell. The froth is skimmed off into a trough; the mineral concentrate is obtained by washing and filtering. The unwanted mineral grains sink to the bottom of the cell and are removed. So the ore in this process is disassembled by means of fine grinding, a water repellent, and soapsuds. A big mill may have scores or hundreds of flotation cells.

Iron ore known as taconite is produced in Minnesota and upper Michigan. Taconite is a hard, dense rock that consists of silica and the iron oxide minerals hematite (Fe_2O_3) and magnetite (Fe_3O_4). It must be upgraded before it can be sent to the smelter. After fine grinding,

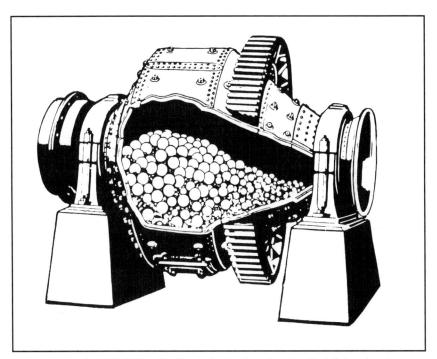

A cutaway view of a ball mill. Crushed stone introduced at the left is reduced to a powder by the grinding action of the balls as the mill rotates. Mills are 8 feet (2.4 meters) or more in diameter.

the hematite and magnetite are separated from the silica magnetically. The concentrate is formed into pellets, for ease in handling and shipping. The pellets contain 60 to 67 percent iron.

Ore minerals may be separated from waste on the basis of gravity, solubility, or several other properties. Optical sorting equipment can even separate minerals by color, reflectivity, or fluorescence.

The third stage of metal production—after mining the ore and concentrating the desired minerals—is refining, to obtain the metal itself. Sulfide ores, such as those of copper, lead, zinc, and molybdenum, are heated, or roasted as they say, to drive off the sulfur. The molten metal is poured into molds and cooled to form bars for the final user. Sulfurous fumes from this process, once a major pollutant, are no longer allowed to escape to the atmosphere; indeed, today's smelters are a major source of commercial sulfur.

Pelletized taconite and other forms of iron ore are mixed with limestone and heated in a furnace. The limestone combines with silica and other impurities in the ore. It forms a scum, or slag, which is drawn off separately from the molten iron. The iron, in the form of bars or "pigs," is ready for use in making steel. The slag, when cooled and hardened, is crushed for use as aggregate in concrete.

To produce alumina from bauxite involves two steps. Both are complex, and both are expensive because of the energy needed. In the first step, bauxite is refined to yield alumina, Al_2O_3. In the second, metallic aluminum is produced. A large and constant supply of energy is required. To make 1 pound (0.45 kilogram) of aluminum from about 5 pounds (2.3 kilograms) of bauxite uses electricity equal to burning a 1,000-watt light bulb for six hours. Remelting of aluminum containers takes only 5 percent as much energy. Recycling clearly makes sense.

Coconut shells and a deadly poison would seem to be unlikely substances to meet in a gold refinery. Nevertheless, both are used in an elaborate process by which the gold of the Carlin Trend (Chapter 3) is recovered. Gold will combine with very few substances, but one of them is cyanide (a poisonous compound of carbon and nitrogen with potassium, KCN, or with sodium, NaCN). Another substances that gold finds attractive is roasted coconut shells (activated carbon). The process starts with finely ground ore in a solution of water and cyanide and ends with metallic gold.

A week's activity at a gold refinery may produce one bar, about the size of a shoebox, of gold plus a little silver that was present in the ore. The bar will weigh about 1,000 ounces (28,300 grams).

Producing Oil

An oil well is drilled by a steel bit at the bottom of a length of steel pipe, called the drill string, which is turned by machinery on the drilling rig. The bit bores through rock layers just as a carpenter's bit bores through wood. As the well gets deeper, more lengths of drill string are added. Wells more than 20,000 feet (6,100 meters) deep are not uncommon.

The ground-up rock at the bottom of the hole must be removed, and the bit has to be lubricated and cooled. So, while drilling is going on, a fluid is pumped down the drill string, through holes in the bit, and back to the surface between the drill string and the walls of the hole. The drilling fluid carries the rock cuttings to a pit beside the rig, where they are removed before the fluid is recirculated. The most commonly used drilling fluid is a mixture of water and a clay called bentonite.

Sometimes the bit encounters open fractures or other very porous zones. Then the drilling fluid is drained away. To combat this "lost circulation," as oil men call it, materials are sent down the well to plug the openings. These materials range from cottonseed hulls to shredded money—dollar bills routinely destroyed after wearing out.

One of the techniques that have been developed is drilling at an angle, so as to reach a part of the oil pool many hundred feet away

An unusual use for dollar bills: introducing shredded, worn-out money into a core hole. It plugs cavities in the rocks encountered by the drill, stopping the loss of drilling fluid.

from a point directly below the rig. This directional drilling is much used in offshore oil production, as drilling platforms are very expensive to build and maintain. All or most of an oil pool may be reached from a single platform.

Offshore drilling, in as much as 1,000 feet (300 meters) of water, poses many problems in regard to supply, housing, storage, safety, pollution control, and related matters. But once the bit enters the seabed, procedures and techniques are much the same as on land. Reservoirs of oil and gas are no different beneath the sea than they are beneath the land. The rock layers are continuous, onshore and offshore.

The rate of oil production ranges from a few barrels to many thousand barrels per day. (A barrel is 42 U.S. gallons, 35 imperial gallons in Canada, or 159 liters.) In 1929, a well in the Yates pool of western Texas had an official production rate of more than 200,000 barrels per day. This may be a North American record, but such rates are commonplace in the Middle East.

The gusher—the popular image of great wealth, as crude oil or black gold erupts unchecked from a well—wrecks the rig, wastes oil, wastes reservoir pressure, and messes up the countryside. Worst of all, a gusher may become a roaring inferno if a stray spark sets it afire. If high pressures are to be expected in a drilling well, a heavy blowout preventer may be installed on the rig. Or the drilling fluid may be weighted with ground barite, a mineral more than four times as heavy as water. Flowing wells, yielding oil under control, are desired, but gushers are to be avoided at all costs.

Some oil wells flow because gas is dissolved in the oil under pressure. When the reservoir rock is penetrated by the drill, the oil surges upward, just as soda pop fizzes out of the bottle. Other wells flow because of water pressure in the rocks below the pool.

You can recognize a completed flowing well by a "Christmas tree"—a pipe sticking up out of the ground with many branchlike valves and fittings. A pumping well is revealed by a "pump jack," an A-frame supporting a beam that moves up and down like a seasaw. A well drilled for oil or gas that didn't find either one is a dry hole, even though it may have encountered water. Dry holes are filled with cement.

Wells are connected by gathering lines to field storage equipment. The oil and gas will be separated and if necessary will be "scrubbed" to remove sulfur. The gas is then ready for the pipeline to market, and the oil for pipeline or tanker to the refinery.

Here's a surprise: when the average oil pool has been exhausted, first by flowing, then by pumping, more than 50 percent of the oil remains in the reservoir rock. How can this be? A petroleum engineer puts it this way: "Imagine a cubic foot of undisturbed reservoir rock. Locked into its tiny pores may be a gallon of oil and half a gallon of water. If rolled into a flat plane, the surface area of its millions of rock grains could be as much as 50 acres. There you are, with a wet surface equal to about five football fields over which is dispersed a gallon of oil. Your job is to skim up as much of it as you can. That is the oil recovery problem." Engineers have developed some methods of increasing total recovery, but the problem of "oil left in the ground" is a serious one.

5

Mineral Resources and the Environment

Opening up a rock quarry or a mine, or drilling a well for oil, might seem like a simple straightforward operation. There are, however, many factors involved. It is especially important to consider the impact that such operations have on the surrounding community and on the environment.

Rocks in the Community

The Agmix Stone Company went into business in 1950 to supply crushed stone for the concrete needed in the nearby city. Its quarry was 8 miles (13 kilometers) from the center of town and 3 miles (5 kilometers) from the outer fringes. The city grew and the company prospered. Also, the suburbs expanded. In fact, one of them approached and finally surrounded the Agmix property.

Because the company's activities are dusty and noisy and must be carried on right out in the open, the nearby residents consider the site a bad scene. Besides a big hole in the ground, there are immense piles of rock material and structures of heavy machinery—all presided over by rough-looking men in hard hats. Dump trucks roar in and out. The company owns land adjacent to the quarry, for future expansion. Local builders would like to acquire this land for residential development.

So the town fathers are constantly urged to require this intolerable nuisance to move away. The fact that Agmix's product is essential to the community's growth is ignored.

A city government cannot close down such a business in one day, but it can do it in a year or two. The process is called zoning. This just means designating certain parts of the community for certain purposes. The business section is zoned commercial, the parks are zoned recreational, and so on. At a meeting, the zoning board may vote to change the rating of the Agmix property from industrial to residential. The company is then

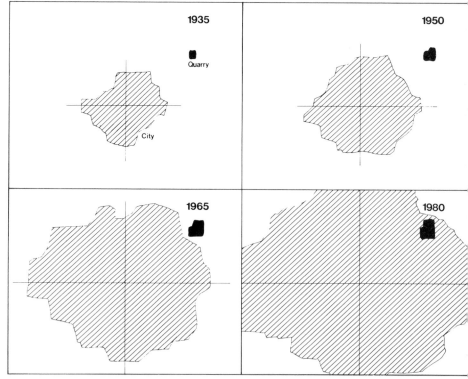

A crushed-stone quarry, well out in the country when it was established, is now inside the city limits. Neighbors object to the noise, dust, and truck traffic.

38

informed that it has become a "nonconforming use." It has, say, eighteen months in which to close out its operations, sell its property, and move away.

The quarry may be landscaped for a park or lake, and the adjacent property will make nice home sites. The Agmix Stone Company, if it stays in business, will have to find another deposit, farther away from town.

Sometimes good deposits of gravel or stone are sealed off from use because a highway or housing project is built on them. Thus the expanding community, which increases the demand for aggregate, may cover the land that could supply it. Natural terraces along a river are more likely to be used as building sites than as sources of sand and gravel.

In many places, reclamation of worked-out areas is standard practice. A large gravel pit in the San Fernando Valley of California became a site for trash disposal in 1953. By 1970, it was filled to the original ground level, and the property was sold for approximately $21,000 per acre. Former gravel pits in southern Ontario have been landscaped for schools and playgrounds. In the east-central United States, many gravel deposits are below the water table. After the gravel has been removed by dredge or clamshell bucket, the area forms a pond or lake. Companies have found that advance planning will yield property that sells for more than they paid for the land, even though they removed aggregate in the meantime. Or a company can earn goodwill by donating such property to the community for a park. Former rock quarries make attractive municipal parks and gardens.

Ore Deposits: Three Histories

Urad Valley, Colorado, lies in the Rocky Mountains about 45 miles (70 kilometers) west of Denver. The valley floor is at 9,800 feet (3,000 meters) above sea level; Red Mountain, just to the north, rises to more than 12,300 feet (3,700 meters). Beneath Red Mountain a large deposit

The Royal Botanical Gardens, Hamilton, Ontario, Canada. This is a former limestone quarry, as shown by ledges in right foreground.

of molybdenite was discovered. Mining started in 1967; by 1974, the ore body was depleted and mining ceased.

Molybdenite (MoS_2) is the chief ore of the metal molybdenum, which is used as an alloy in steelmaking. The ore from the Urad mine was milled on the property. Molybdenite concentrates were shipped east for refining.

From the beginning, the mining company looked toward eventual reclamation. The greatest problem was in the disposal of waste rock, or tailings, washed from the mill. This waste was guided to two ponds constructed on the valley bottom. Here the solids settled out, and the water was recovered for reuse. The filled ponds had to be covered with crushed rock to keep the tailings from blowing away, and fertilizers such as sewage sludge and wood waste were added to promote plant growth. Problems were numerous. The growing season was short. Wildlife consumed some of the plants introduced. Every seedling of spruce had to be protected from direct sunlight to keep it from being killed by ultraviolet rays. Reclamation and studies of environmental factors are expected to continue till 1996. Total to be spent on the Urad Valley reclamation project will exceed $7,700,000.

Mining and milling here, as at most mines, have injured the land surface and natural ecosystems. But the area is small: slightly more than one-third of a square mile, or about 88 hectares. What is unusual is the mining company's interest in environmental matters and its willingness to spend money and manpower on minimizing the damage done in obtaining 48.5 million pounds (22 million kilograms) of metallic molybdenum.

What environmental problems are faced by a company that wishes to start a new mine?

In 1966, a mining company found a large phosphate deposit on government land at Pine Mountain in southern California. The deposit is about 90 miles (145 kilometers) west-northwest of Los Angeles. In 1969, the company applied for a mining lease.

As the deposit is in the Los Padres National Forest, the company worked closely with the United States Forest Service. It complied with all government regulations, and the proposed mine received approval by the Environmental Protection Agency. At a public hearing, however, some nineteen organizations expressed strong opposition. Not only would the mine be on the public domain, but it would lie in the flying and soaring corridor of the California condor. This bird has been declared a rare and endangered species.

The company presented detailed plans for handling water and soil problems, for disposing of wastes, and for reclaiming the land. But these plans received little attention. Rather, opponents focused on recreational land use and wildlife conservation. These needs were felt to outweigh the need for earth-derived resources. The phosphate deposit remains undisturbed; no lease has been granted.

In the early 1970s, a major deposit of vermiculite was discovered in northeastern Virginia some 50 miles (80 kilometers) from Richmond. All property is privately owned. When a company announced that it planned to open a mine in 1980, it stirred up a hornet's nest among landowners.

Vermiculite is one of the mica group of minerals. On sudden heating, particles expand to as much as twenty times their original volume. Expanded vermiculite is used as insulation and soil conditioner.

Interest centered in the Green Springs area of prosperous and historic farms. To allow mining, the land would have to be rezoned, from agricultural to industrial. Some owners favored rezoning and wished to lease their land for mining; others emphatically did not. After more than two years of deadlocked board meetings, public hearings, lawsuits, and court orders, the zoning board voted in favor of mining. But the original company withdrew. Another company has opened a small-scale mine. As with the California phosphate deposit, opposition did not center on practical matters. Opponents simply stated that mining would be "intrusive and disruptive" and they did not want it.

A lost mineral resource in suburban Denver, Colorado. The upper photo was taken in 1938. The landowner's request to remove sand and gravel from the indicated area was denied because nearby residents protested. The owner then sold the property to a developer. The lower photo, taken in 1965, shows same tract after houses were built. The sand and gravel will never be extracted.

Oil—the Environmental Problem Child

Early in the morning of March 24, 1989, a supertanker called the *Exxon Valdez* struck rocks in Prince William Sound, Alaska, and spilled 11 million gallons of oil into the sea. Winds spread the thick black oil southwestward, destroying or damaging wildlife and fouling many miles of shoreline. Clean-up efforts, which were expensive and lasted for months, were only marginally successful. Effects of the spill will be felt in Prince William Sound for a long time.

This spill is by no means the only major one in recent years. In 1967, the tanker *Torrey Canyon* was wrecked near Land's End, England; about 36 million gallons of oil was washed onto British and French beaches. In 1978, the *Amoco Cadiz* lost seven times as much crude oil as the *Exxon Valdez,* in a wreck off the coast of France. Routine ship operation and minor accidents spill millions of gallons of oil into the ocean each year.

Supertankers are essential in getting the world's crude oil from where it is found to where it is needed. The *Exxon Valdez* was carrying oil from Alaska to California. A fleet of similar vessels moves oil from the Middle East, North Africa, and Venezuela to the United States, western Europe, and Japan. These are enormous ships: more than 1,000 feet (300 meters) long, 175 to 200 feet (50 to 60 meters) wide, and extending 79 feet (24 meters) below the water surface when loaded. Supertankers cruise at only 14 or 15 knots (about 17 miles per hour) and are very difficult to maneuver. In incompetent hands, or at close quarters on an unfriendly coast, they are accidents waiting to happen. But the world must have the oil carried in these giant ships.

Drilling a well for oil or gas seems to be done without regard for the immediate surroundings. A bulldozer prepares the site. Big trucks haul in the derrick, drilling platform, and drilling machinery. Storage racks for drill pipe and casing are set up. A shallow pit is dug to collect rock cuttings brought up in the drilling fluid. Trucks and cars make ruts in the area around the rig. Altogether, the effect is much like the preparation of a site for a big new building.

Come back in a few weeks, after the well has been completed. Derrick, drill pipe, and machinery are gone. The pit has been filled in and the area graded. If the well was successful, it shows as a pipe with several valves and fittings, the so-called Christmas tree; or a big pump marks the site. If the well was a dry hole, all that is left is a low cement-filled pipe. There is a neat enclosure and a sign giving the oil company's name, the name of the landowner, and the well number. What at first appeared to be a gross disruption of the environment turns out to be limited in area, limited in time, and not so gross after all.

Offshore drilling is a more risky operation. On January 28, 1969, an oil and gas blowout occurred at an exploratory well being drilled in the Santa Barbara Channel, southern California. About 840,000 gallons of oil, and much natural gas, were lost in the ten days before the well could be shut off. It turned out that the pool was shallow— within about 300 feet (90 meters) of the seafloor—and contained very high pressures. The pool is in an area where the earth's crust is unstable and is cut by fractures and faults. Indeed, natural seepages of oil into the sea are common along this stretch of coast.

At a formal inquiry into this spill, it was decided that the best procedure would be to produce the pool's oil and gas as rapidly as possible, thus reducing the excessive pressure. From three platforms, thirty-eight wells were drilled with no environmental problems. By January 1975, the field had produced more than 100 million barrels of oil and 51 billion cubic feet of gas.

Worldwide, there are hundreds of offshore drilling rigs. They are operated with great care, to assure the safety of crews and the stability of the platforms. Some pollution is unavoidable, but sizable spills are very rare.

Environmental Impact

For a couple of centuries, the mining industry had things pretty much its own way. People needed its products, and no one paid much attention to the impact of mining on the environment. Since about 1960, however, environment-conscious sectors of the public have made themselves heard. New federal and state agencies have set forth regulations that must be met. Public hearings on proposed new mines or mine extensions have become standard procedure.

As a result, the mining industry has been placed on the defensive. Indeed, a sort of either/or, you-or-me attitude has often developed between the industry and the community. Industry leaders tend to view environmentalists as impractical dreamers, more interested in preserving beautiful views and rare fish than in obtaining essential earth materials. Environmentalists tend to look on mining companies as greedy despoilers of the landscape, insensitive to its beauty or wildlife.

There is no standard procedure by which friction can be avoided. Each proposal must be considered on its own. Sometimes the community prevails, as we saw in the case of the California phosphate deposit. Much depends on the company's attitude—on whether it will deal up front with the community, as one quarryman phrased it. When a company proposed to open a limestone quarry in Alabama, the company's management declined to meet with concerned citizens. At a public meeting, only the legal department appeared. The quarry was turned down. A gravel company in the upper Midwest requested a permit to relocate a stream—and then went ahead and relocated it without waiting for permission. As the waterway is a cold-water trout stream, the company not only defied the state department of natural resources but also angered the area's fishermen. This is a fine example of how not to develop community support.

On the other hand, some company proposals are successful. An aggregates concern received permission to open a large pit near a town in southern California—but only after agreeing to build a community golf course when the gravel was removed. Other approvals by a community may involve "sweetening" the agreement by requiring the company to reclaim the property after mining, as a park or lake area. All such permissions and agreements require good-faith bargaining and a willingness to compromise.

Not all environmental impact is felt near cities. A large underground mine in Montana, opened in 1987, has been praised by the United States Forest Service and even some conservationists for its sound environmental planning. Only 15 miles (24 kilometers) north of Yellowstone National Park, the mine produces platinum for use in automobile emission-control systems. This mine merely emphasizes the fact that the days of wide-open, let-it-rip mining are long gone. Reclamation of strip-mined areas, controlled disposal of mine wastes, and protection of air and water are all part of the earth-resource picture today.

6

How to Look at the Future

Since 1982, gold has been mined from 2,100 feet (640 meters) below ground at a place just 65 miles (100 kilometers) from the Arctic Circle in the Northwest Territories of Canada. In the summer, the ground is melted to an impassable mud, and the only access is by air. In the winter, trucks drive 370 miles (600 kilometers) from the nearest town; 70 miles (112 kilometers) of this distance is on frozen ground and the rest on the ice of lakes. It is hard to imagine a worse location for a mine.

Why would anyone locate a business at such a spot? Answer: Mining companies have no choice. Gold is where you find it. Some is below the Arctic wastes, some is in the Nevada desert, some is 5,000 feet (1,500 meters) beneath the surface in South Africa. Of course, what is true of gold is also true of other mineral resources. Oil companies, for example, don't drill wells in the stormy North Sea or on the bleak north coast of Alaska by choice; they drill there because that's where the oil is. Much as we might wish it otherwise, the world's mineral resources are distributed by the rules of geology, not by human preference.

The scattered or sporadic occurrence of mineral resources is one of the factors that make the mineral industry different from the manufacturing industry. A manufacturer may locate his factory wherever he wishes, to take advantage of a growing market, a good labor supply, or other factors. A mining company cannot do that.

For any given mineral resource, there are "haves" and "have-nots" among nations. The United States is rich in the ores of iron, lead, and copper, and in sulfur and salt. But we must import 70 to 75 percent of our zinc, tin, nickel, and chromium; and practically all our ores of aluminum and manganese. All our industrial diamonds come from overseas. International economics and politics enter the picture here. Most of the world's chromium reserves, for example, are in South Africa and the U.S.S.R. This situation makes chromium a politically sensitive metal. Minerals that are considered to be vital to the security of a nation but that must be procured mostly or entirely from foreign sources are termed strategic minerals. The ores of chromium and tin, among others, were designated strategic minerals during World War II. Some governments, including that of the United States, maintain a stockpile, or reserve supply, of certain minerals to guard against future shortage or emergency.

Obviously, no mineral deposit lasts forever. Sooner or later every deposit is exhausted, or mined out. Western ghost towns remind us of this fact. So a mining company, in the ordinary course of business, uses up its capital stock. To compensate the company for the fact that it is consuming, or depleting, its capital, a certain percentage of the company's income from its producing properties is exempt from federal income tax. This depletion allowance varies. For iron ore, for example, it is 12 percent; for oil and gas, 15 percent.

This exhaustibility of deposits is another contrast between mining and manufacturing. If a factory runs low on its raw material, the manager simply orders more from his supplier. The miner has no such option. The manufacturer may worry about labor problems, taxes, or markets. The miner worries about reserves—that is, the supply of ore that is still to be mined. If a company's ore reserves are low or approaching exhaustion, all other problems cease to matter.

Reserves and Resources

Reserves are defined as deposits of known size and purity—proven deposits—that can be profitably produced at existing prices with existing techniques. A reserve may consist of tons of rock, tons of ore,

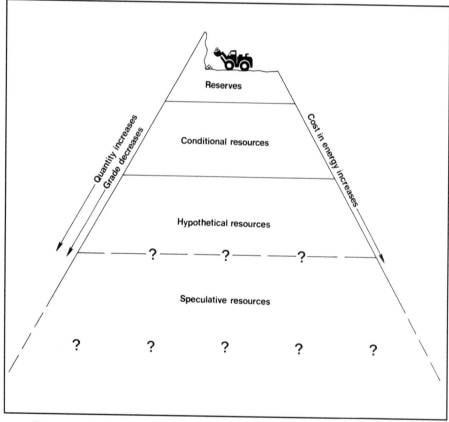

Reserves and resources. The big triangle represents the total amount of a given mineral resource in a region or country. Reserves (at top) can be profitably mined today. Lower-grade conditional resources may become reserves through a rise in price, a technical breakthrough or a relaxation of environmental requirements. Hypothetical resources are believed to exist in a known district; speculative resources are just that.

barrels of oil, or cubic feet of gas. Resources, on the other hand, constitute the total amount of a given material in the earth's crust, or in that part of the crust that is being considered. Resources include reserves. They also include conditional resources—deposits that have been evaluated but cannot be mined at present for political, economic, or technical reasons. The California phosphate deposit described in Chapter 5 is a good example of the conditional resource. Hypothetical resources may be expected to exist in favorable districts. Speculative resources, which may exist in unexplored districts, are the most "iffy" of all.

Reserves interest mining companies, but resources interest governments. Every modern country must have an inventory of its mineral fuels, metals, and industrial rocks and minerals. The more accurate the inventory, the better the planning that can be based on it. Should the government stockpile chromium ore in case of emergency? Should it grant producers of natural gas special tax or depletion treatment? Should it encourage offshore exploration for sand and gravel? To answer such questions with assurance, the government must have good information on the total resources of each earth material. It must know how much is currently recoverable as reserves, how long these reserves will last at present rates of production, and what types of resources are available for future use.

Some of our mineral resources are widely distributed and essentially infinite. We will never run out of salt, limestone, silica sand, clay, or gypsum. But, as we have seen, many other earth materials occur in limited amounts and in unpredictable places. If a company is in the business of mining one of these resources and wishes to remain competitive, it must maintain an exploration staff. This group of geologists has the task of locating extensions of the deposit being mined or of finding new deposits altogether. It was smart geological reasoning that discovered Nevada's rich Carlin Trend gold deposits, discussed in Chapter 3. A company's long-run success depends on discovering and acquiring reserves well ahead of need.

Oil companies tend to support exploration more vigorously than mining companies. As we have seen, there is good reason for this attitude: oil deposits are hidden. It is very difficult to locate new pools, especially the big ones that make a significant addition to the world's supply. Sophisticated geological and geophysical exploration is essential.

There is a second way to increase reserves. This is to modify or improve the methods of treatment of raw material, so that lower grades can be used; in other words, to convert formerly useless rock into ore. An example is provided by kaolin, a white clay mined in Georgia. The development of a high-intensity magnetic separator, which allows the removal of the last traces of iron-bearing minerals from the clay, has added millions of tons of formerly unusable kaolin to our total reserves. Another example is the iron ore of northern Minnesota and Michigan. The high-grade hematite and magnetite ore was long ago exhausted, but techniques have been developed for fine grinding, magnetic separation, and the forming of pulverized ore into pellets for handling. These have made available enormous tonnages of low-grade siliceous ore, or taconite (Chapter 4). Engineers in companies' processing and metallurgical divisions make such advances possible.

Petroleum engineers have developed methods of increasing oil recovery by repressuring the reservoir rock. Work continues on the thorny problem of how to recover the oil that stubbornly clings to the reservoir pores and so remains in the ground after the pool has been depleted. A success along this line will tremendously increase oil reserves.

Some people view technology as the hope of the future. If technological advances make it possible to use lower and lower grades of earth material, they say, eventually we will be using common rocks and seawater. Indeed, it is possible today—though wildly impractical—to obtain aluminum from granite and gold from the ocean. A scenario something like this one may develop in the next century for some of the metallic ores. For these, technology is potentially more important than exploration. A new discovery, it is said, adds an ore deposit; but a new technology may add to ore deposits all over the world.

Alternatives

Aluminum cans, copper wire, and lead batteries may be reclaimed and their metal used again. Recycled or "scrap" steel is a significant part of the steel industry. But recycling meets only a fraction of the total needs for these metals. For most mineral resources, furthermore, recycling is not a possibility at all. Stone, coal, oil, gas, sulfur, and other earth materials are taken out of circulation with a single use. They go around only once, so new supplies must constantly be developed.

Producers of crushed stone for urban markets have to be situated close to point of use, but must not use too much land or degrade the environment. Where geologic conditions are favorable, a producer may find it profitable to turn to underground mining. Costs are high, about 30 percent of the rock must be left in the ground as supporting pillars, and the size of equipment is limited. On the other hand, there are year-round operations, independence from weather, minimal requirements for surface space, and no overburden or waste to be handled. Between 5 percent and 10 percent of the total output of crushed stone comes from underground.

A valuable byproduct of underground mining is the space that is left when mining is completed. Such space has been converted to cold storage, warehousing, manufacturing, and keeping of archives and computer records. Costs are low, foundation problems are nonexistent, noise and vibration are at a minimum, and the facility is fireproof. Also, the cost of heating, air conditioning, and freezing is much lower than with installations on the surface.

The floor of the sea is a potential source of mineral wealth. From

From limestone quarry to room-and-pillar mine to underground storage facility. North Kansas City, Missouri.

A former limestone mine, modified for secure storage of companies' tapes, disks, and other back-up computer records. This room is half a mile from the entrance and 80 feet below the surface.

time to time, news stories tell of vast areas covered with metal-bearing lumps or nodules, which may be scooped up and brought to the surface. Typically the nodules consist of iron and manganese oxides, with small amounts of nickel, copper, and cobalt. Phosphate-rich nodules have also been found. All these materials lie on the floor of the deep ocean, as much as 3.75 miles (6 kilometers) below the surface. Their recovery poses awesome problems of engineering and expense, and commercial mining is not likely for many years.

Of much more immediate interest are deposits of sand and gravel that lie on the continental shelf in less than 300 feet (90 meters) of water and within a few miles of the coast. These deposits are receiving attention from producers of aggregate who have been "zoned out of business" on the land, especially in the Boston-New York urban corridor. Less than 30 miles (50 kilometers) off Massachusetts Bay is a deposit containing one billion tons of sediment that is at least 60 percent gravel. This deposit, at 160 to 320 feet (50 to 100 meters) below sea level, could readily develop into a major source of supply for the greater Boston area and neighboring communities. Another such deposit lies just off the coast of New Jersey, at a depth of only 60 to 130 feet (10 to 40 meters).

In mid-1989, the Minerals Management Service of the United States Department of the Interior announced final prospecting regulations for such offshore deposits. Regulations for leasing and for further activities were expected to appear later in the year. Particular attention is being paid to environmental matters. Opportunity for public input and cooperation with adjacent states are included in the regulations.

It is likely that offshore dredging of sand and gravel will begin in the United States in the early 1990s. Other countries have been in the business for many years. Forty percent of Japan's building sand comes from offshore deposits. In the United Kingdom, 15 percent of all the sand and gravel aggregate comes from the seabed.

Much oil and gas are produced from deposits that happen to lie below the seabed rather than below the land surface. Offshore rigs are at work in seaways such as the Santa Barbara Channel off California, the Gulf Coast of the United States, and the North Sea between England and Norway. In 1989, the world's tallest offshore rig was installed in 1,760 feet (540 meters) of water, at a point about 100 miles (160 kilometers) off the Louisiana coast. There is no doubt that offshore deposits of oil and gas will be important for a long time to come.

The continent of Antarctica is a potential source of mineral wealth. How much is there and how it can be exploited are unknown quantities. Oil and gas are probably present, large deposits of coal are known, and metallic sulfide minerals have been identified. Severe problems stand in the way of development, however. About 98 percent of the continent is ice-covered and so to all intents and purposes is not accessible. The climate is as harsh as any on earth, and distances to market are great. Legal and political problems also exist. Antarctica has long been administered by an international treaty, mainly for scientific study. In mid-1989, the twenty nations who signed the Antarctic Treaty adopted a plan for prospecting, exploring, and developing mineral resources. This plan limits drilling depths, requires permits for development, and sets up procedures to avoid pollution of the fragile Antarctic environment. To be activated, the plan must be signed and ratified by sixteen member nations. It is probable that commercial exploitation of Antarctic mineral resources will not take place till the mid-1990s at the earliest.

Mineral resources on the moon are entirely speculative. Any lunar activity would have to start with life's necessities: oxygen, hydrogen, and water. How these would be obtained, to say nothing of other resources, is at present a subject for science fiction.

Glossary

aggregate—Sand, gravel, or crushed stone, mixed with cement to form concrete.

anticline—An arch or upward fold in sedimentary rocks.

concentrates—The valuable part of an ore left after worthless material is removed in processing.

core drilling—Drilling with a bit that cuts a ring-shaped hole, allowing a cylinder of rock to be recovered for examination.

depletion—The gradual exhaustion of an ore deposit or oil pool as a result of production.

directional drilling—The drilling of multiple oil wells from a single location, such as an offshore platform. Each well is drilled at a controlled angle and in a known direction.

dry hole—The oil industry's term for an unsuccessful well.

fault—A fracture in the earth's crust, along which the rocks on one side have been displaced with respect to those on the other.

igneous rocks—Rocks that result from the cooling and solidification of molten earth material, such as lava.

lode—A mineral deposit consisting of a group of veins or other ore-bearing units; a mineral deposit in consolidated rock, as contrasted with a placer.

metamorphic rocks—Rocks formed from preexisting rocks by heat, pressure, and chemical changes deep in the earth's crust.

mineral reserves—Bodies of rock from which a mineral or fuel can be extracted at a profit under existing economic conditions and with current technology.

mineral resources—Mineral reserves plus all other mineral deposits that may eventually become available—known deposits that are not currently recoverable, as well as deposits that have not been discovered but may be inferred to exist.

oil—A naturally occurring complex liquid compound of hydrogen and carbon that can be distilled and purified to yield fuels, chemicals, and lubricants. Also known as petroleum.

oil pool—A body of porous and permeable rock below the ground surface that contains oil in economic quantities.

overburden—Worthless soil or rock lying on top of a near-surface mineral or rock deposit. It must be removed as mining proceeds.

ore deposit—A body of rock from which one or more minerals, generally metallic, can be obtained commercially.

ore mineral—The part of an ore deposit that is economically desirable. It is separated from waste material in processing.

pinch-out—The termination or end of a bed of rock or a vein that becomes progressively thinner in a given direction until it disappears and the rocks that formerly separated it are in contact. Some oil pools are found where porous and permeable sandstone layers pinch-out between impermeable layers of shale.

placer—A mineral deposit consisting of sand or gravel that contains grains of a heavy mineral such as gold. The common types are beach placers and stream placers.

processing—Crushing, grinding, magnetic separation, or other treatment by which an ore mineral is separated from the worthless minerals with which it occurs.

reclamation—The restoring of a strip-mined or quarried area to useful condition.

reservoir rock—In an oil pool, the porous and permeable rock that contains the oil.

room-and-pillar mining—A system of mining in which the rock or ore is removed in rooms separated by pillars of undisturbed rock that support the ceiling.

salt dome—A column of salt that has pushed its way upward from a salt bed as much as 30,000 feet below the surface. Pushing through the overlying sediments, the column arches these layers into a dome. Sometimes these arched layers are reservoirs for oil and gas.

sedimentary rocks—Rocks formed by consolidation of clay, sand, shell fragments, or other sediment; or from the precipitation of dissolved salts from a water body that dries up.

seismic prospecting—The use of artificially generated shock waves to yield information on rocks underground. It is especially useful in exploration for oil.

strip mining—Mining at the earth's surface, in which the valuable rock or ore is exposed by removing the overburden. Coal, stone, phosphate rock, and other materials are mined in this way.

tailings—The waste material produced in the processing of ore.

trap—Any underground geologic feature that acts as a barrier to the upward movement of oil or gas, allowing them to accumulate in a pool.

vein—A mineral filling of a fault or other fracture in rock, commonly in tabular or sheetlike form.

well log—A graphic record of the rocks encountered in a drilled well. It may be made from a geologist's examination of well cuttings or cores, or it may be a record of the rocks' electrical resistivity, radioactivity, or other property.

wildcat well—A well drilled for oil or gas in a new or unproven area, far from established production.

zoning—Designation of certain areas of a community for certain purposes, such as residential, commercial, or industrial.

Further Reading and Information

Further Reading

Bates, R. L. *Industrial Minerals: How They Are Found and Used.* Hillside, N.J.: Enslow Publishers, Inc., 1988.

Bates, R. L. *Mineral Resources A–Z.* Hillside, N.J.: Enslow Publishers, Inc., 1991.

Bates, R. L. *Stone, Clay, Glass: How Building Materials Are Found and Used.* Hillside, N.J.: Enslow Publishers, Inc., 1987.

Bates, R. L., and J. A. Jackson. *Our Modern Stone Age.* Los Altos, CA: Kaufmann, 1982. Available from American Geological Institute, Alexandria, Va. 22302.

Boatright, M. C., and W. A. Owens. *Tales from the Derrick Floor.* New York: Doubleday, 1970.

Dorr, Ann. *Minerals—Foundations of Society,* 2nd ed. Alexandria, Va.: American Geological Institute, 1987.

Fodor, R. V. *Gold, Copper, Iron: How Metals Are Formed, Found, and Used.* Hillside, N.J.: Enslow Publishers, Inc., 1988.

Kesler, S. E. *Our Finite Mineral Resources*. New York: McGraw-Hill, 1976.

McDivitt, J. F., and G. Manners. *Minerals and Men*. Baltimore: Johns Hopkins University Press, 1974.

Pampe, W. R. *Petroleum: How It Is Found and Used*. Hillside, N.J.: Enslow Publishers, Inc., 1984.

Seabrook, John. "Invisible Gold." *The New Yorker*, April 24, 1989.

Scott, E. *Doodlebugging: The Treasure Hunt for Oil*. New York: Warne, 1982.

U.S. Bureau of Mines. *Mineral Facts and Problems*. Washington, D.C.: U.S. Bureau of Mines, Bulletin 675, 1985.

Utgard, R. O., G. D. McKenzie, and D. Foley. *Geology in the Urban Environment*. Minneapolis: Burgess, 1978.

Wallace, R. *The Old West: The Minerals*. New York: Time-Life Books, 1976.

Young, B., and J. Young. *Gusher: The Search for Oil in America*. New York: Messner, 1971.

Further Information

American Geological Institute, 4220 King Street, Alexandria, VA 22302.

American Mining Congress, 1920 N Street NW, Suite 300, Washington, DC 20036.

American Petroleum Institute, 1220 L Street NW, Washington, DC 20005.

Minerals Information Office, Department of the Interior, Room 2650, 18th and C Streets NW, Washington, DC 20240.

National Stone Association, 1415 Elliot Place NW, Washington, DC 20007.

Index

About the Author

Robert L. Bates is Professor Emeritus of Geology at Ohio State University. He is a founder of the annual Forum on Geology of Industrial Minerals.

Dr. Bates has written a number of articles and books, and edited the *Dictionary of Geological Terms*. His young adult titles for Enslow Publishers, Inc. include *Stone, Clay, Glass: How Building Materials Are Found and Used* and *Industrial Minerals: How They Are Found and Used*. He is also the author of *Mineral Resources A–Z* in the Environment Reference Series.